The Monster Within

by
Darryl S. Brister

The Monster Within

by
Darryl S. Brister

PUBLISHING · INC

Tulsa, Oklahoma

Unless otherwise indicated, all Scripture quotations are taken from *The King James Version* of the Bible.

The Monster Within
ISBN 0-9657706-7-2
Copyright © 1998 by
Darryl S. Brister
P. O. Box 1526
Harvey, LA 70059-2526

Published by PHOS PUBLISHING, INC.
P. O. Box 690447
Tulsa, OK 74169-0447

The Monster Within

Until now monsters have usually been found in the movies. Monsters have been fictionalized characters from plays, books, screen plays or movie scripts, but I am here to tell you, today there is a monster that is real. It is not the product of someone's creative, artistic mind.

You have a monster of your own. It is living on the inside of you and rears its ugly head at every opportunity. Since Adam and Eve were booted out of the Garden of Eden, every human being has been born with a personal monster within.

Paul revealed his monster and dealt with it in the book of Romans. Let's look at his words and find some hope for conquering the monster that lives within each of us.

For we know that the law is spiritual: but I am carnal, sold under sin. For that which I do I allow not: for what I would, that do I not; but what I hate, that do I. If then I do that which I would not, I consent unto the law that it is good. Now then it is no more I that do it, but sin that dwelleth in me. For I know that in me (that is, in my flesh,) dwelleth no good thing: for to will is present in me; but how to perform that which is good I find not. For the good that I would I do not: but the evil which I would not, that I do. Now if I do that I would not, it is no more I that do it, but sin that dwelleth in me. I find then a law, that, when I would do good, evil is present with me. For I delight in the law of God after the inward man: but I see another law in my members, warring against the law of my mind, and bringing me into captivity to the law of sin which is in my members. O wretched man that I am! who shall deliver me from the body of this death? I thank God through Jesus Christ our Lord. So then with the mind I myself serve the law of God; but with the flesh the law of sin.

**Romans 7:14-25**

A sad thing has happened to us as Christians. Somewhere along the line we have chosen to relate to God through our emotional and material instincts. In church we relate to God from our emotions. On the outside of the church, people dictate your spiritual condition by the number or worth of the blessings God has given you; and on the inside, the church also judges you by the clothes you wear, the car you drive and the house you live in.

But you know what I found out? I discovered that in the Body of Christ you can be wearing a $3,000 Brioni suit and be messed up on the inside. You can have on a $2,000 St. John knit dress and not feel worth two cents on the inside.

I want you to take a few moments with me just now to go on a little journey.

Let's go where no one else can go but God. Let's go on the inside — the inside of your mind, your will and your emotions.

Everything that you do in your daily life affects the anointing that God has placed upon you for godliness and service to Him. I believe that the anointing of God is available for everyone. The only person who can short-circuit the anointing in your life is *you*.

It is critical to understand that your real enemy is not that snake, Satan. It is not your husband who is a lazy good-for-nothin' bum. It is not those children who don't have enough sense to come in out of the rain. It is not your wife who will never listen to you and spends all your money. Your real enemy is not your parents who neglected you and never gave you any encouragement to succeed.

Your enemy is that big bundle of

humanity that is thriving, resisting, and desiring to control you from the very core of your being. It is camouflaged by gender, attributes, and personalities.

Paul Had a Monster

Paul's life and ministry have a powerful impact on us today. This man was used by God to write over two-thirds of the New Testament. Paul sat at the foot of Gamaliel and learned about the things of God from this celebrated Rabbi doctor and teacher.

His spiritual journey was not all based on emotions, though it was certainly birthed in an emotional experience. If you remember, God was so anxious to get hold of Saul, that he was encountered in a dramatic way.

Saul was on his way to Damascus with letters that would allow him to prosecute Christians when a light from heaven flashed around him. He was knocked to the ground, slain in the Spirit by God alone. God asked him directly why he (Saul) was persecuting Him (by persecuting His children). When Saul asked who was speaking, the voice answered, "I am Jesus, whom you are persecuting."

All those around heard the sound, but did not see anyone. Saul could not see for three days and when he arrived in Damascus, he did not eat. He had a vision of a man named Ananias, and so he called for him.

Ananias feared Saul. He knew what had been done to his fellow believers because of this man. But God spoke to Ananias and assured him that He had chosen Saul, whose name would be changed to Paul, to carry His name before Gentiles and kings.

Then God added one little postscript in speaking to Ananias, one we often choose to overlook. The Lord told

Ananias, "I will show him how much he must suffer for My name."

Ananias was obedient and went to minister to Saul. As he did the blindness left. It was as if scales just dropped off Paul's eyes. He was baptized, ate and once he had gained his strength, he began to learn from the disciples and to give his testimony in the synagogues, declaring that Jesus was the Son of God.

Paul was anointed and appointed by God. He was chosen, and had an emotional but life-changing experience with God. However, in the text from Romans we see a different side of Paul. We see deep inside his flesh.

Some theologians debate this particular passage of Scripture. Some say this is not the situation of a real child of God. I've even heard great studies of the law, and I have read how many have insinuated that what Paul was relating here was not anything that happened *after his salvation experience* but it is about what was going on inside him before he surrendered to God.

That's an easy way to dismiss this important passage. We could just agree with these great theologians. On the other hand, I believe we wouldn't be reading any Holy Ghost inspired text that would bring us confusion. Paul was not confused about any other time in his life, because he knew that those sins of the past had been forgiven.

Here in this passage from Romans, Paul is reflecting on the law that is spiritual but given to carnal man who is "sold unto sin." Paul was addressing the issue of his greatest enemy — the enemy within.

I too must recognize that my real enemy is "in-a-me." We are constantly at war within ourselves. We are daily contending (fighting) for our faith to remain strong, thereby causing us to make the right choices.

Maybe you can't relate to what Paul and I deal with. Maybe we are not as spiritual as you. It is amazing to me that most Christians go to church and look like they are on the mountaintop. They seem to be fasted up, prayed up and have a fresh word or revelation from the Lord. If the truth be told, often what we see on the outside is not what is really going on inside.

It's Time To Tell the Truth

I guess we preachers are somewhat at fault, because when we present the Gospel, very seldom do we share with the new convert initially that some days are going to be rough days even though they are now saved.

> These things I have spoken unto you, that in me ye might have peace. In the world ye shall have tribulation: but be of good cheer; I have overcome the world.
>
> John 16:33

Just imagine how many people would come to the altar if we told them that. "Beloved, first you must give up everything that means anything to you. You must stop doing all the things you love to do. You must be willing to go without and die for Christ if necessary, but if you don't die soon, then you will have a life of suffering many things for the cause of Christ. Come forward now and receive Jesus as your Lord and Savior." That is the full Gospel and the true Gospel, not in a doctrinal sense but literally.

Instead, we offer them the good side of God, the sins forgiven and washed away in the-sea-of-forgetfulness speech. The glorious promise of eternal life is real and offers hope to the downtrodden, but it is not the full story.

The truth is they will have years of dealing with one real big monster: The one living within that they will have to slay on a daily basis to live victoriously in the Kingdom of God at present and forevermore.

I wish I could follow you around your house or your office or your job for one day, then I would see the real you. The not-so-victorious, dealing-with-everyday-issues, struggling you!

It is easy to be holy in the church. We know how to talk the talk. We know how to talk about God's goodness. It is easy to get jerks and bumps while we are on the inside of a sanctuary and the music is blaring and the choir is swaying.

Every person reading this book has a monster on the inside. You may be looking good on the outside, sitting up in first class of an airplane looking all spiritual reading this book. You may be surrounded by your laptop computer, your cell phone and your pager and look like a prosperous professional. You may be all dressed up and looking fine, but on the inside of you there is a monster and this monster won't leave you alone.

It is a shame to say that when you go to some churches you have got to put on airs or you have to pretend in order to fit in. Paul said that there was a war going on inside of him. And inside of you the battle is raging.

Now that no-good, mean devil goes to church too. He won't wait until you leave church to plant some destructive device in the fertile ground of your mind. He has a mine field there and it doesn't take much to get you to step on one memory that will trigger an explosion in your thoughts. Some of your most negative thoughts will break through right while you are in church — things you have no business thinking about. Yes, there is a monster in you and in me that we must deal with.

Your flesh will rise up and want attention just at the point of the pastor's most profound revelation. You may look like you are drinking it all in and taking notes in your spiritual journal, but instead your flesh is writing out your grocery list, planning your week, or writing a letter to someone you have no business writing to.

We need to go inside and look at our real self. We must take off those robes and collars and drop the titles and positions because those things are not really you. The real you is the one who comes out when there is nobody else around. That's the monster on the inside of you.

Paul told Timothy, "For if a man know not how to rule his own house, how shall he take care of the church of God?" (1 Timothy 3:5). And the same Paul said to the church of Corinth, "What? know ye not that your body is the temple of the Holy Ghost?" (1 Corinthians 6:19).

God showed me something with these passages. He says it's not just about ruling the place of your domicile, where your address is, but you've got to learn how to bring distress under control and rule the house — your body, the temple of the Holy Ghost. It's about how I rule my own house.

There are theologians who try to take the easy way out of this because they say that Paul could not have really been dealing with the new man, because over in chapter 8 and verse 1 he talks about the new man. Theologians argue that this is a total contrast and Paul could not have been referring one moment to the flesh and then the next moment to the spirit.

But you know I beg to differ with that situation, because if we think about real life, that's exactly how we live real life. One moment you can be so spiritual and feel His presence and anointing, and the next moment you're thinking about something that you ain't got no business thinking about.

If you want the real, pure anointing of God on your life and you want it to flow freely in your ministry, you will have to deal with the monster within. We have to grab the enemy by the tail and yank him out of our lives.

The life of a saint, the life of a born-again believer, is a blending of spirituality and carnality. We don't like talking about this in the church, because when you think about it, the whole Christian walk is a paradox. God often calls you to do things and to say things that really don't make sense.

The Lord has been showing me that we need to begin to market the Gospel another way. We need to begin to let that new convert know the whole story. We need to lay our titles and our positions aside and be real. I'm not where I am today in ministry because I've been so good. I'm not where I am because I don't ever mess up.

People see us with our titles and positions rejoicing and shouting in church, but we aren't always like that, because every one of us deal with some of the same things.

> Humble yourselves therefore under the mighty hand of God, that he may exalt you in due time:
>
> Casting all your care upon him; for he careth for you.
>
> Be sober, be vigilant; because your adversary the devil, as a roaring lion, walketh about, seeking whom he may devour:
>
> Whom resist stedfast in the faith, knowing that the same afflictions are accomplished in your brethren that are in the world.

> I Peter 5:6-10

It doesn't matter who you are. You can try to look sophisticated and deep, but if the truth were to be told, you are made of the same stuff that everyone else is made of. It doesn't matter if you are anointed or not, you've still got to deal with that monster.

> **Behold, I was shapen in iniquity and in sin did my mother conceive me.**
>
> **Psalm 51:5**

I know you have been in church for a few years and I know you probably speak in tongues. The Lord has probably used you to prophesy to other folks, but just for one moment, get real — do you see yourself in Romans 7?

You've got to deal with it, you've got to deal with your flesh. The Lord has been showing me that in order for you to get what He has for you, you've got to go through what you are going through.

I don't know what your interpretation of the particular text is, but this is what I want you to do just for a moment. Take a minute and reread that passage, then honestly see if you can relate.

Do you see yourself? If we are honest, we are all there. Paul says, "For that which I do I allow not: for what I would, that do I not; but what I hate, that do I... In my flesh, dwelleth no good thing" (Romans 7:15,18).

As New Testament believers we don't enjoy talking the way Paul did. We like to let people think that we are always on the mountaintop, and that every time the devil shows up we rebuke him and he goes running off.

If the truth is to be told, there are some things that we have done in our lives that we're glad our fellow Christian brothers and sisters don't know about. And might I say, I'm not talking about things we've done before we got saved, or just when we were a new Christian. What about two weeks ago?

Paul said, "In me...dwelleth no good thing" (Romans 7:18). In me — myself — there is no good thing. The only good thing about me is God in me, the hope of glory. Without Him in me, there is only me in me, and in me there ain't no good thing!

Now I want to ask you something, because I have to preach the whole Gospel. Why in the world would God make you rich without changing you inside, because all you would be is a dressed-up, prosperous monster! The bottom line is, there is nowhere in Scripture where you will ever see written, discussed, or discovered that a saint won't have to struggle.

I'll tell you this, I have found out there is only one sure way that you can live above sin. You have to live in a two-story apartment with people underneath you who don't go to church. Now you're living above sin!

This is the thing that really gets me, because this is the paradox of the whole issue. Nowhere in the Bible does it say a saint won't struggle, yet this is how we govern our whole lives. You can't find where it says a saint will not struggle, but the church is the very last place you can be honest enough to tell somebody you're struggling.

It's a shame because if I can be real anywhere, it ought to be in the church. I ought to be able to get a brother by the hand and say, "Man, I need you to pray with me, because this devil is eating me up on the inside. I need help over this spirit of lust. I need help with this spirit of fornication." But the last place we can confess is in the church.

I heard a story of some elders who went out to pray with a man from their congregation. He was convicted and touched by their concern so he confessed that he struggled with homosexuality and alcohol. They prayed with him and then encouraged him to keep his weaknesses to himself and not to discuss them with anyone else in the church, because they would not understand and they would always judge him by it. Sadly, that is the truth.

Most people find it easier to confess to their bartender or their beautician than to their brother or sister in Christ. The average church is filled with a bunch of hypocrites and pretenders. We're always jumpin' and we're always shouting, but that isn't really what's going on in our lives. If we tell the truth, we will have to let the new convert know that our lives don't always line up with the Word of God.

There are some things that the devil brings across our minds that we know we shouldn't think about, and every time we don't rebuke him instantly the monster takes over our minds. When Jesus was in the garden of Gethsemane, when He was about to go to the cross, He struggled. He struggled with His flesh.

I can hear Jesus saying, "Lord, bid

this cup to pass from Me." You know what Jesus was really saying? Jesus was saying, "Lord, I really don't want to go through this."

We ought to just go on and fess up, take off the masks and stop the music of sanctimony and take off our eyeglasses of pietism for a moment. We need to feel what Jesus felt. Now if Jesus struggled, what in the world makes you think that you won't struggle? I know we've got to struggle.

Instead, we want to stand up and say, "First giving obedience to God, Who is the great Head of the Church. Pastor, officers and members of this church, I would like to tell you, first of all...." That ain't your testimony. If you told your real testimony, half of us would run out of the church and we'd be screaming and hollering, because we never ever would have believed that you've done some of the things that you've done. But the problem is, we can't be real in church.

It's time to be real. Jesus struggled in His flesh. Jesus said, "I don't want to go through this, I know what I'm called to do, but I don't want to go through it." Have you ever felt like that?

> **For we have not an high priest who cannot be touched with the feeling of our infirmities; but was in all points tempted like as we are, yet without sin.**

> **Hebrews 4:15**

You know what God is calling you and instructing you to do, but you don't always want to do it. You knew that He was asking you to give up those old feelings, or the intents of your heart.

You knew He wanted you to arrive at the Marriage Supper of the Lamb without a spot or a blemish. You knew that all He wanted was some of your precious time that day to praise and lift Him up. But sometimes you just don't feel like lifting Him up.

In every trying situation of life, we can overcome the monster within.

> **Ye are of God, little children, and have overcome them: because greater is he that is in you, than he that is in the world.**
>
> **1 John 4:4**

Monster Examples

You don't have to look too far back in Scripture to find people who were dealing with their monsters. David had a monster. On one occasion when all his men went out to war, David stayed home. He was a little weary of war so he thought he'd take a break. He was walking out on the rooftop wallowing in his boredom when he spied Bathsheba.

Now he should have gotten on his horse and headed for the camp of his men. Instead, he rode straight into the arms of trouble, because he allowed the monster within to take possession of his senses.

He knew how to cry out to God for direction or for help. He had relied upon it when he faced the lion and when he faced the bear. I guess when he came face to face with this "fox," however, he didn't want to be delivered. He didn't want God's help with that monster within.

Samson had a monster within. He had been set apart from birth, anointed as a Nazarite for Kingdom service. He was marked by God and given physical strength and wisdom for the purpose of defeating the Philistines. But he had a monster within.

His own passions took control and cost him his strength, wisdom, sight and then his life — but most of all, the monster within robbed him of his anointing. Who knows just how much Samson would have accomplished and how differently the story would have turned out if only he could have conquered the monster within.

King Saul, David's predecessor, had a monster. His real enemy was the green-eyed envy and jealousy monster, not David who had once been his dearest friend. When Saul could not control the enemy within his own flesh, he became a madman. He pursued David with a vengeance, consulted a witch for guidance and ended his own life. He knew the deliverer. He knew God was responsible for the anointing on David to be king, yet when the monster reared its ugly head, he surrendered to it instead of crying out to God.

Elijah had a monster. This anointed prophet of God had some dramatic miracles. He spoke the word of the Lord to the prophets of Baal and then proved with fire from heaven every word he had spoken. Not long after that great victory, he became afraid and ran.

Elijah allowed the word of one woman to trigger his monster within. He almost gave in to the monsters of despair, depression and defeat when he prayed to die because he just didn't feel he could take any more of life's challenges.

So far in these men of God we have seen battle weariness, lust, envy, jealousy, depression and fear manifest themselves as monsters, destroying everything they could.

Men, however, are not the only ones tripped up by monsters within. The same monsters haunt and hound women, too, because many of them are anointed of God. A lying snake caused Eve's monster to respond. She had forgotten that she was already created in the image of God, so when she was tempted to be like God, her pride and envy monsters rose above reason.

Sarah's monster was doubt. She doubted God would really be true to His Word, so she concocted her own plan for childbearing. Her doubt and unbelief monster created a circumstance that has continued to wreck havoc down through the ages between the Arab and Israelite people.

Naomi struggled with the monster of bitterness. Hannah, Samuel's mother, struggled with self-pity. Esther struggled with her race. They all had monsters to overcome in their ongoing walk with God.

Victory Over the Monster of Circumstance

You can give glory to God when you don't understand the circumstances. You can tell the world how you were delivered from temptation. (Before, you were too holy to even admit to being tempted!) God can receive glory as a result of a humble and honest attitude.

One sister had just put her mother in a nursing home. She was angry at God, because the Alzheimer's disease had not been healed and God had not provided the finances for her to quit her job and stay home and care for her mother full-time. She could have allowed resentment toward other family members to raise its ugly head and roar loudly in the circumstances. She was angry at the medical workers who saw her mother as only a sack of bones and flesh, when she knew what a great woman of God she was.

But in the end, God got the glory. Instead of throwing a fit at everyone, and saying a lot of hurtful things that would never be forgotten, she walked out into the beautiful fresh air, looked up into the billowy blue sky and said, "God, You know I don't like this one bit — not any of it — but I trust You!"

She had a grip on the monster inside of her. She knew that her true strength could only come from God and for years, because she overcame, she was able to offer help and hope to others in the same circumstance.

Can you imagine how anointed we would be if every one of us would take the mask off and be real? I'm about to go through another level. I'm about to get a fresh anointing now, because I'm going to deal with this monster on the inside of me — in-a-me! I'm going to deal with this monster on the inside!

Have you seen yourself in any of these heros of faith? Scripture does not record it, but I am sure that Abraham must have struggled a little with unbelief when God told him to take the child of promise and lay him on the altar of sacrifice.

When Joseph finally faced his brothers after twenty-two years[1] of hardship because of their evil deed, he granted them mercy. You see, Joseph had dealt with the monster of revenge. He had faced down the monster of rejection and had continued in faithful service to God in spite of the monstrous situations life had brought his way.

Recognize Your Monsters

Where are you in your struggle with your monsters? Have you recognized them? Do you know what trips your trigger and unleashes their poison in your life?

I know you are probably saved and sanctified, but if the truth were to be told, when you are alone in your room, you can't even get away from the phone. You know you shouldn't pick it up, you know you don't need to call him, but something on the inside of you makes you call and now you find yourself spending time with somebody you aren't even attracted to. They don't even look like two cents. But because you're so lonely on the inside, that monster rises up and takes charge.

You know you should forgive that one who did you wrong so long ago and yet you can't wait for the day when they get what is coming to them. You lay awake nights scheming to get even.

You may not even be certain what your monsters are, but you know you are not happy. You respond to many things in anger and then wonder where that came from. God can help you discern it and then help you overcome it, if you are willing to submit yourself totally to Him.

Get a Grip on Your Monster

Right now wherever you are, lift your feet. Now, put them back down and say, "Devil, you're under my feet now. God is going to give me the power to conquer every one of these struggles in my life."

This is not the type of message that we like hearing in church. We like to hear the man of God promise us that everything is going to always be all right. But you need to know that the flesh is a mess. While you are reading this thing right now, some of you are thinking about sexual sin.

That is not the only sin of the flesh. Some of us gossip too much and need to take control over our flesh. If you can't push away from the table and fast and pray, you need to take authority over your flesh. Each one of us is dealing with something on the inside. There is a monster just waiting to rear its ugly head and cause you to sin.

Many of you are sick and tired of struggling. Every time you take one step forward, the devil knocks you two steps backward by triggering that monster within.

God told me to tell you that He will increase your anointing, but you cannot lose the agony and gain the destiny, unless you go through what you're going through. But when God gets through with you, you shall come forth as pure gold. He will give you the power to go through victoriously.

My Prayer for You

Father, right now, this instant, as we pray together I know You hear us. If we are in our kitchen or on an airplane, You see us and know the intents of our hearts.

My brother or sister in the Lord is hurting today. They have discovered the monster within and they want to be delivered. They want to operate in the full anointing You have given them. Help them today to know how to have victory over their flesh — the monster that continues to rise up and control them.

Give them wisdom for every day and every decision. Show them how to die daily — how to stop the monster each time it chooses to make itself known. Give them victory today.

Help my dear brother and sister to make the right decision. Show them how to build themselves up in their most holy faith. Show them how to strengthen and build up their resistance to the monster within. And finally, Lord, renew in them that glorious hope that one day we will all be like You. We will have overcome for the last time and we will rule and reign with You free from the pull of the old sinful nature.

Thank You, Lord, for meeting us now. We need You today and every day, and we will rely on You daily to help us in conquering the monster within.

[1]Dake, Finis Jennings. *Dake's Annotated Reference Bible*. Lawrenceville, GA: Dake Bible Sales, Inc., 1963, 1991, O.T. p.45.

Pray With Me

If you are in a private place just now as you are reading this, simply lift your hands and begin to cry out to God. If you are in a public place and are not ashamed, go ahead and tell the Lord how much you need Him:

Lord, I need You to protect me, I need You to cover over every one of my weaknesses. I need Your anointing and whatever it takes for me to be anointed. I will make myself available for Your power.

Tell Him you are sick and tired of the same old struggles. Cry out for deliverance in the name of Jesus. Call upon His power to deliver you from the monster within. Come boldly to His throne and throw yourself at His feet. Admit all your human frailties and give yourself to Him all over again.

Tell Him you are willing to do whatever it takes to have victory over the monster in your flesh. Repent for listening to the voice of the enemy over the voice of God that is trying to direct you in the right path. Beg for His mercy and ask for a fresh touch from Him. Accept His forgiveness and His power to overcome, and let yourself be wrapped up in the freshness of His anointing that is coming upon you now, in Jesus' name.

Pray for a Friend

Now pray for someone else. Remember, Job got the victory when he prayed for his friends. Pray that they will be released from their enemy within. Release them in the Spirit to allow the Lord to have His way in their life.

Praise God for All He Has Done

Now call someone you respect and trust in the things of God and tell them you are free. Give God all the glory and the praise for allowing you to overcome the monster within.

God's Promise to You

The Lord told me to tell you that He will increase your anointing, but you've got to give yourself totally to His usage. He may not come when you want Him to come, but He's always on time!

> O wretched man that I am! who shall deliver me from the body of this death?
>
> I thank God through Jesus Christ our Lord. So them with the mind I myself serve the law of God; but with the flesh the law of sin.
>
> There is therefore now no condemnation to them which are in Christ Jesus, who walk not after the flesh, but after the Spirit.

For the law of the Spirit of life in Christ Jesus hath made me free from the law of sin and death.

For what the law could not do, in that it was weak through the flesh, God sending his own Son in the likeness of sinful flesh, and for sin, condemned sin in the flesh:

That the righteousness of the law might be fulfilled in us, who walk not after the flesh, but after the Spirit.

Romans 7:24 - 8:4

Biography of
Bishop Darryl Sylvester Brister

Bishop Darryl Sylvester Brister was born in New Orleans, Louisiana, on September 26, 1966. He received his license to preach in 1989 and was ordained on May 1, 1992, under the administration of Bishop Paul S. Morton, Sr.

He is married to Dionne Flot Brister and is the father of four children: Darrlynn Lanor, Darryl Sylvester, Jr., Dariel Soterio, and Trey Darius Brister.

He attended Central Texas College, The School of the Prophets of Copperas Cove and Union Baptist Theological Seminary of New Orleans.

On March 10, 1989, he was elected as Pastor of the Camp Red Cloud Gospel Service in Uijongbu, Korea. Bishop Brister has ministered the Word of God in several countries such as Japan, Holland, Korea, Iceland, and Europe.

Since July, 1993, Bishop Brister has served as Senior Pastor and Teacher of the Beacon Light Missionary Baptist Church, located in the city of New Orleans, Louisiana. He received a Bachelor of Theology Degree from McKinley Theological Seminary in December of 1993. He has an anointed calling on his life which has caused the congregation to surpass 6,000 faithful members, and he has incorporated several seasonal institutes and revivals, nurtured numerous community outreach programs, and implemented 50 active in-house ministries.

On January 26, 1996, Bishop Brister was elevated to the highest position in the church, the office of a "Bishop." He was the youngest ordained Minister, at the age of 29, to be called to the office. In the Full Gospel Baptist Church Fellowship, he serves as the Bishop of Adjutancy.

Bishop Brister's leadership abilities have been recognized throughout the world. In his most recent set of accomplishments, he was featured in the 1995 November edition of the *Ebony* magazine as one of the "Top 50 Leaders of Tomorrow." Much of Bishop Brister's teachings are known for revealing through Christian principles the known tactics of every Christian's enemy — Satan. He has authored another book entitled, *Exposing the Enemy*.

Bishop Darryl S. Brister is a committed and motivated man of God. He has a deep hunger for winning souls for Christ. He is committed to serving God, dedicated to follow wherever God may lead and excited as God continues to do "A Brand New Thing" within his life and ministry.